Sports Marketing in the Age of Social Media

Table of Contents

In the future, there will be no female leaders. There will just be leaders.

Chapter 1. Introduction

In the vibrant world of competitive sports, an exciting revolution is unfolding. Our Special Report, "Sports Marketing in the Age of Social Media," digs deep into the thrilling intersection of two dynamic domains, showcasing how they are reshaping each other. Following the exciting journeys of brands, athletes, and teams, we navigate through their strategies and experiences in the rapidly evolving landscape of social media. Whether you are a marketing veteran hoping to up your game, or a sports enthusiast curious about the behind-the-scenes action, this comprehensive report will be your essential guide. With engaging narratives, insightful analysis, and practical tips, it will kindle both your passion and knowledge. Your journey into the exhilarating world of sports marketing is just a click away. So, be ready to be inspired, educated, and entertained. Step into the ring, it's game on!

Chapter 2. Introduction to Sports Marketing in the Social Media Era

To truly comprehend the significance of what is happening in the world of sports marketing in today's age, it's crucial to first understand what it looked like before the advent of social media. Before the digital revolution, sports marketing was a venture that leant heavily on traditional broadcasting channels such as television, radio, and print press. The distribution of news, updates, and promotional content was largely unilateral, leaving limited room for fans to interact directly with teams or athletes. In this system, marketers controlled narratives, and passive consumers were left only to absorb them.

2.1. The Dawn of Digital Media

Following the turn of the millennium, the world of communication saw drastic transformations sparked by the web's advancement. As the new medium burgeoned, so did opportunities for sports marketing. Digital platforms offered an interactive environment where engagement with fans could materialize in real-time. Moreover, accessibility to a broader audience suddenly seemed more feasible. Despite these prospects, many were initially skeptical, skeptical about the longevity and impact of online marketing in sports.

Then came the true game changer - social media. Websites like Facebook, Twitter, and later Instagram, opened a world of unprecedented possibilities for building brands and amplifying reach. The instantaneous exchange of information, direct interaction with fans, real-time feedback and trend tracking have offered a dynamic shift from conventional marketing.

2.2. Understanding Sports Marketing in the Social Age

Today, sports marketing through social media extends beyond mere promotions; it is about building relationships. Brands, teams, and athletes are now capable of having direct dialogue with their fans. This paradigm shift brings an imperative need to understand this complex, interactive, and rapidly changing environment's nuances.

Derived from the amalgamation of sports and digital communication, this marketing strategy encompasses everything from audience targeting to content creation and dissemination. It is carried out on various platforms, including Facebook, Twitter, Instagram, LinkedIn, and even TikTok, each offering unique features and reaching different demographics. Experimentation and adaptation have become central tenets of a successful online sports marketing campaign in this landscape.

It's important, however, to note how this intersection of sports and social media is not just transforming marketing strategies, but is also reshaping the sports industry itself. The ability to present oneself directly to the public has given unprecedented power to athletes in carving their digital personas. Teams, concurrently, are creating identity beyond their physical locality, enabling fan loyalty stretching across geographical limitations.

2.3. Challenges in This New Era

Although social media provides a promising avenue for sports marketing, it doesn't come without its share of challenges. With the enormous amount of content produced every second on social media, standing out becomes difficult. Another major obstacle is the necessity for rapid response times. Fan queries or criticisms left unanswered can lead to backlash or public relations issues. There's also a risk of content misinterpretation, leading to potential controversy.

Yet another challenge is the constant need to be on top of new trends and technologies. In the ever-evolving universe of social media, staying relevant requires staying informed and updated. This fast-paced digital evolution may demand additional resources in terms of time, personnel, and money.

2.4. Opportunities Ahead

Regardless of its challenges, the potential of social media in sports marketing remains untapped. Live streaming, immersive technologies such as virtual and augmented reality, and sophisticated data analytics tools present exciting future possibilities. The ability to react instantly to trends and shape narratives in real-time is a powerful tool in the hands of sports marketers. Utilizing these technologies, they can provide personalized, interactive fan experiences that can foster deeper connections leading to loyal fanbases, and ultimately, a more successful sports franchise.

In conclusion, sports marketing in the social media era is a new frontier filled with challenges and opportunities. It requires adaptability, creativity, and a deep understanding of both sports and digital landscapes. It demands a shift in traditional thinking towards more fan-centric tactics. The endgame is not merely to sell, but to create lasting relationships and memories. The mutually beneficial dynamic between the sports entities and their fans brought forth in this new era opens a new chapter of unprecedented opportunities in sports marketing. The journey has only begun, and it promises to be an exciting one. As the curtain lifts on the social media era of sports marketing, only the most innovative and agile will win in this evolving game.

Chapter 3. The Evolution of Sports Marketing: A Historical Overview

The story of sports marketing is a sweeping narrative that not only reflects the evolution of the sports industry, but also the societal changes and advancements occurring over time. Driven by a potent blend of sporting passion, commercial considerations, technology advancements, and shifts in consumer behavior, the trajectory of sports marketing is as thrilling as the sports it serves to promote and augment.

3.1. The Dawn of Sports Marketing

The origins of sports marketing can be traced back to the late 19th and early 20th centuries, coinciding with the rapid growth of sporting events and the rise of mass media. During this era, sports were growing in popularity, reaching large audiences through radio broadcasts and print media. Businesses began to realize the commercial potential of associating with these mass-attended sporting events. They started sponsoring events and teams, leveraging the emotional connection between fans and sports to increase their brand visibility and reach.

Early sports marketing efforts were simple by today's standards, primarily focusing on creating visibility through logos and signage during games or leveraging popular athletes' images for product endorsements. Sports like Baseball and Boxing saw the beginnings of wholesale merchandise like jerseys and equipment, while athletes like Babe Ruth became household names due to promotional endorsement deals with consumer goods companies.

3.2. Television and its Transformative Impact

The advent of television marked a significant turning point in the world of sports marketing. As live sports got beamed directly into households, and the televisual spectacle drew millions of eyes to the screen, marketing and advertising found a captive and highly engaged audience.

The live and highly unpredictable nature of sports made it an irresistible draw for viewers, and marketers rushed to capitalize on this new media opportunity. Billions of dollars were poured into high-stakes TV advertising during sports broadcasts, and lavish sponsorships, particularly during marquee events like the Super Bowl or World Series. Also, brands started investing in lucrative endorsement deals with sports stars, yielding iconic campaigns that still resonate today—like Coca Cola's partnership with Mean Joe Green or Nike's association with Michael Jordan.

3.3. Digital Disruption and Marketing Makeover

The dawn of the digital age in the late 20th and early 21st century brought unprecedented changes to sports marketing. With the rise of the internet, followed closely by the emergence of social media platforms, the marketing landscape was revolutionized.

Brands and teams were no longer solely reliant on traditional media to reach their audience. They could now interact directly with fans through their websites, email newsletters, and later, social media channels. The digital era brought about a level of audience engagement and interaction never before possible, transforming fans from passive consumers to active participants.

This period saw the rise of viral marketing campaigns, real-time digital experiences, and branded social media content reaching millions of fans worldwide. Here, sports marketing became less about intrusive advertising and more about creating meaningful, interactive experiences that resonated with fans.

3.4. Social Media: The Game Changer

The emergence of social media as a dominant force in the communication landscape redefined the rules of sports marketing yet again, ushering in what we now know as the era of 'Sports Marketing 2.0'. This new age is characterized by direct, interactive, and two-way communication between sports franchises/athletes and fans.

With channels like Facebook, Twitter, Instagram and Snapchat, sports entities could create a direct line of communication with fans. They could not only share updates, behind-the-scene snaps, player profiles, and more, but also facilitate an interactive space where fans could communicate with their favorite teams and athletes.

A new era of athlete branding rose with social media as athletes could now cultivate their own image and brand. They became influencers with fan-following in millions, signing independently lucrative endorsement deals that rivalled those of their teams. The likes of Cristiano Ronaldo, LeBron James, and Serena Williams are now brands in themselves due to their successful harnessing of their social media presence.

In tandem, sports marketers are now leveraging new forms of content like memes, Stories, and live-streaming, along with user-created content and influencer partnerships, to engage with digital-native Gen Z and Millennial fans. Social listening tools, data analytics, and AI technology are used to fine-tune campaigns, ensuring that messages reach the right audience at the right time through the right channel.

3.5. Conclusion: Beyond the Horizon

As we look ahead, the future of sports marketing promises to be even more exciting with emerging technologies like Virtual and Augmented Reality, eSports, and Blockchain set to redefine the game yet again. As we traverse down this promising path, the continued growth of sports marketing will only be limited by the innovation and creativity of those within its realm.

This historical overview of sports marketing underscores the dynamism that defines this field, and the speed at which it has evolved over just a few generations. From its nascent roots in the early 20th century, to the social-media fuelled frenzy of modern-day sports marketing, this discipline has become an integral part of the wider marketing landscape, connecting brands, athletes and fans alike in an emotion-driven and highly engaging multichannel narrative.

Chapter 4. The Power of Social Media in Sports: An Analytical Deep Dive

As we venture into the depth of social media's impact on sports marketing, it is indispensable to first understand the fundamental mechanisms that drive this intermingled cosmos. Herein, we probe the intricate nuances of this digital playfield, unraveling the elements that power its vibrancy, interactivity, and global reach. This chapter serves as a thorough exploration of the undercurrents that shape and propel the phenomenon of sports marketing in the digital age.

4.1. Unraveling the Social Media-Sports Convergence

Social media and sports have converged into a powerful duo that is transforming the way we perceive and consume sports. The raison d'être of this seamless merger can be linked to social media's fundamental essence. As platforms designed to foster communication, connection, and content sharing, they dovetail perfectly into the social nature of sports.

In essence, sports are more than just games; they represent a collective cultural experience that thrives on fan interaction and engagement. With the advent of social media platforms like Facebook, Twitter, Instagram, and YouTube, these interactions have transcended geographical boundaries, creating a global community of sports enthusiasts. Fans can now connect directly with their sporting idols, engage in discussions, share opinions, and consume exclusive, behind-the-scenes content, all with a few swipes and taps on their smart devices.

Sports entities, be it athletes, teams, or brands, leverage these platforms to build a rapport with their fanbase, foster loyalty, and drive engagement. With every shared post, tweet, or story, they communicate their values, tell their story, and reinforce their brand image. This two-way interaction facilitates a deeper emotional connection, fueling not only fan devotion but also their propensity to purchase, paving the way for potent marketing possibilities.

4.2. Analyzing Key Benefits of Social Media in Sports Marketing

From fostering fan engagement to driving commercial success, social media's influence on sports marketing is multifaceted. Let's deep dive into its key benefits:

1. **Transcending Geographical Boundaries**: By enabling real-time streaming and updates, social media platforms allow sports games to be accessible globally, dissolving geographical boundaries and time constraints. This opens up new markets for teams and brands, exponentially expanding their potential audience.

2. **Enhancing Fan Engagement**: Social media offers diverse avenues for fan engagement. Interactive features such as polls, quizzes, comments, shares, and live streams get fans involved, making them feel more connected to their favorite teams and athletes.

3. **Boosting Commercial Opportunities**: The vast reach and targeted advertisement capabilities of social media promote sponsorships, partnerships, and merchandising, thus opening up substantial revenue streams.

4. **Enabling Real-time Interaction**: The real-time nature of social media empowers teams and athletes to instantly communicate with fans, whether it's celebrating a victory, acknowledging a

defeat, or simply sharing day-to-day experiences.

5. **Facilitating Co-creation**: Social media encourages user-generated content. Fans can share their game experiences, thoughts, artwork, or memes, becoming active participants in the team's or athlete's brand narrative.

4.3. Social Media Platforms and Their Role in Sports Marketing

Understanding the unique features and user bases of different social networking sites is crucial to harnessing their marketing potential. Let's delve into how the major social media platforms intertwine with the sports marketing milieu:

Facebook remains a dominant force, connecting over 2.8 billion users globally. Its vast demographics and features allow for the broad dissemination of information, making it ideal for sharing team news, schedules, and longer form content like interviews or exclusive articles.

Twitter thrives on real-time updates, well suited for live-tweeting games, delivering score updates, or sharing post-game reactions. Its hashtag feature also enhances discoverability and fosters community creation around specific teams or matches.

Instagram is the hub for visual content. High-resolution images, behind-the-scenes photos, sneak peeks into athletes' lives, and short video clips form the heart of Instagram sports marketing. IGTV and Instagram Live also provide avenues for longer video content and real-time interaction.

YouTube, the video-sharing giant, is often leveraged to showcase game highlights, press conferences, promotional videos, or even athletically themed web series. Its community-building tools like comments, likes, and shares further aid in fostering fan engagement.

TikTok is the new player that teams and athletes are quickly integrating into their digital strategy. Its short-form, dynamic content intertwined with music, dance, filters, and effects offer a unique, novel way to connect with younger demographics.

4.4. The Analytics Angle: Measuring Social Media Impact

The efficacy of social media efforts is quantified through robust analytics tools these platforms offer. Let's break down some key performance indicators (KPIs) in sports social media marketing:

1. **Reach and Impressions**: These numbers reflect how many people have seen a particular post or ad. They help understand the potential size of the audience.

2. **Engagement**: This measures how many people interacted with a post, including likes, shares, comments, and clicks. High engagement usually signifies resonant content.

3. **Follower Growth**: Keeping track of follower numbers allows teams and athletes to gauge their growing popularity and influence.

4. **Website Traffic**: Social media can act as a funnel directing fans to official websites where they can access deeper content or make purchases.

5. **Conversion Rate**: This metric calculates how many social interactions lead to desired actions such as merchandise purchases, ticket sales, or sign-ups for newsletters.

In conclusion, the critical examination of social media's role in today's sports marketing landscape undeniably points to its unprecedented power. It's an arena where the action is now as fervent off the pitch as it is on it, and where the cheers of the crowd are echoed with likes, shares, and comments. Armed with the insights gathered in this in-depth dive, let's venture forth into the fascinating journey of how athletes, teams, and fans navigate this digital playfield, build their personas, master these platforms, and redefine sports marketing's future contours.

Chapter 5. The Player's Persona: Building Athlete Brands on Social Platforms

In today's social media-dominated age, the development of an athlete's brand, as you likely already know, extends far beyond sweat-soaked jerseys and explosive plays on the field. With an audience of billions globally, social media platforms have unlocked unprecedented opportunities for athletes to meticulously craft their persona, connect with fans on a personal level, and monetize their popularity. This chapter aims to peel back the layers of how athletes can leverage the potent power of social media to create a persona that resonates with fans and fortifies their brand value. Let's delve into this invigorating journey armed with robust understanding, diversified perspectives, and strategic insights.

5.1. Establishing the Base: Understanding the Power of Persona

Athlete branding, at its core, is about shaping public perceptions and forging emotional bonds with fans. The narrative begins with the definition of 'persona', a concept that refers to the perceived public image of an individual. For an athlete, their persona is a potent amalgam of their on-field performance, off-field behavior, values, personality traits, personal style, and social media activity. In turn, this persona dictates fan engagement, sponsorship opportunities, and an athlete's overall marketability.

Where does social media fit into all these? It has been a game-changer, offering athletes a direct, unfiltered channel to showcase their personality, values, and lives, impossible with conventional media. It has transformed athletes from distant, larger-than-life figures to relatable human beings.

5.2. Crafting the Persona: Strategic Steps and Considerations

As the first step towards building a persona, athletes need to introspect and define who they are and what they stand for. Clarity on their values, passions, and unique traits forms the bedrock of a consistent and authentic persona. Next, understanding their target audience, their preferences, sensibilities, what they value in their sports heroes, is crucial. This is followed by adopting a distinctive communication style and content strategy aligned with their persona and audience expectations.

Athletes must also maintain a healthy balance between showcasing their sporting prowess and offering glimpses into their personal lives, balancing professionalism with relatability. Regular, consistent engagement, rapid response to comments and messages, and adept handling of trolls and negative comments are all part and parcel of effective persona management on social media.

5.3. The Role of Content: Crafting Stories that Resonate

Content is the currency of social media. Setting apart from the crowd demands not just high-quality content, but content that envelopes the athletic persona within compelling narratives. Whether it's a behind-the-scenes training video, a congratulatory post for a teammate, a charitable endeavor, a candid family photo, or a fun brand endorsement, each content piece should encapsulate the athlete's persona and tell a story that resonates with fans.

The utilization of various content formats - posts, stories, reels, IGTV, etc., novelty in content treatment, and adequate visually appealing elements are also key to ensure content diversity and engagement. Embracing trends, memes, and challenges humanizes the athlete, bringing them closer to their fans and making them relatable.

5.4. Managing Risks and Challenges

While social media offers immense benefits, it also opens athletes up to risks - every post, every tweet is a potential contention source. Careful, conscious communication is a must. Athletes also need to manage the incessant scrutiny and deal with trolls and negativity without losing their cool. Social listening tools can help in early identification and mitigation of potential PR issues.

5.5. The Reward: Monetizing the Persona

Once a strong, engaged follower base is established, various monetization avenues open up for athletes - from sportswear collaborations, sponsored posts, and endorsement deals to exclusive content on subscription platforms and personalized fan merchandise. The key is to ensure that any endorsements or collaborations align closely with the athlete's persona, values, and the perceived authenticity is maintained.

To wrap up this detailed exploration, building an athlete brand on social media is as much about strategic prowess as it is about authenticity and keeping fans at the center of all efforts. The payoffs, however - a deeply engaged fan base, increased marketability, and lucrative monetization opportunities - are well worth the meticulously strategized and executed journey. The power is in the hands of the players, let's see how they play it!

Chapter 6. The Team's Triumph: Mastering Social Media for Sports Franchises

In the rapidly evolving landscape of sports, franchises are no longer solely dependent on on-field performances to win over fans and boost their bottom line. Social media has emerged as a game-changer, unlocking new avenues for sports franchises to engage with their audience, build brand love, and expand their consumer base. This chapter delves into the strategies and techniques employed by leading sports franchises to master social media and harness its full potential.

6.1. The Social Media Ecosystem: An Overview for Sports Franchises

To begin with, let's explore the ecosystem of social media. Comprising several platforms, each with its unique characteristics, social media presents wide-ranging opportunities for sports franchises.

Facebook, with its massive user base, is a goldmine for driving mass interaction and engagement. Instagram, featuring rich, vibrant media, is the go-to platform for showcasing behind-the-scenes action, player snippets, and match highlights. Twitter serves as the pulse of live sports conversation, fostering real-time dialogue with fans. LinkedIn, although overlooked, can highlight the franchise's thought leadership, CSR initiatives, and business stories. Understanding these platforms' unique strengths and audience demographics is crucial to chalk out a robust social media strategy.

6.2. Strategy Formulation: Crafting the Winning Game Plan

Creating an effective social media strategy is akin to devising a successful game plan. It requires understanding the fans, defining the goals, and leveraging the appropriate channels and content to engage the audience.

Listen to Your Fans: Every successful social media strategy begins with understanding the audience – their preferences, behaviors, and how they interact with your brand on various platforms. In-depth fan analysis and social listening tools can serve as the cornerstone, providing actionable insights to enhance fan engagement.

Set Clear Goals: Sports franchises must chalk out clear, measurable goals that are aligned with their wider marketing and business objectives. These could range from increasing fan engagement, expanding global reach, driving merchandise sales, to promoting CSR initiatives.

Leverage the Right Channels & Create Compelling Content: Picking the right social platforms and creating tailored, compelling content, ranging from text, images, videos, live streams, podcasts, to AR (Augmented Reality) and VR (Virtual Reality) experiences, can foster deeper connections with fans.

6.3. Player Promotion: Harnessing Star Power for Brand Building

Players are the lifeline of sports franchises. By amplifying their endeavors on and off-field, teams can espouse their ethos, tap into fans' emotional connections, boost brand perception, and drive engagement.

Spotlights on Players: Teams can post player profiles, interviews, workout routines, and behind-the-scenes footage to personalize player narratives.

Real-time Coverage: Live-posting about player performances during the game can create real-time frenzy, propelling fans to react, comment, and share, driving exponential online reach.

Involving Players in CSR Activities: Showcasing players' involvement in franchise-led CSR initiatives can invoke fans' emotional ties, fortifying the team's brand image.

6.4. Product and Merchandise Promotion: Driving Sales Through Social Media

For franchises looking to monetize their social media presence, merchandising offers tremendous opportunities. Leveraging social media's e-commerce features, teams can turn their followers into customers.

Showcasing Merchandise: Teams can leverage visually rich platforms like Instagram to showcase their merchandise, creating mini-lookbooks that appeal to fans' aesthetics.

Utilizing Shoppable Posts: Today, many social platforms offer shoppable posts - users can view product details and proceed to purchase without leaving the platform. This seamless experience can boost conversion rates.

Offering Exclusive Discounts and Offers: Exclusivity creates urgency! Offering discounts and offers exclusive to social media followers can drive impulsive buys and increase sales.

6.5. Measuring Success: Keeping Track of the Social Media Scoreboard

Given its dynamic nature, it's imperative for sports franchises to keep track of their social media performance. Insights gleaned from analytics can help fine-tune strategies, optimize campaigns, and achieve superior engagement.

KPI Tracking: Earned media value, impressions, reach, engagement rate, conversion rate, and ROI are some KPIs that can help teams measure their social media effectiveness.

Competitive Analysis: Benchmarking against competitors can offer valuable insights and inspire creative ideas to enhance social media strategies.

Fan Sentiment Analysis: Beyond numbers, understanding fans' sentiments, appreciations, and complaints can guide teams in chalking out their future course of action or managing crisis situations.

6.6. Conclusion: The Road Ahead for Sports Franchises

As the line between the physical and virtual worlds blurs, social media will play an even more significant role in shaping sports franchises' future. From AI-driven personalized fan experiences to the rise of e-sports and VR-enabled immersive viewing, there's vast untapped potential awaiting exploration. At the heart of it all, understanding fans, innovating relentlessly, and fostering authentic connections will remain crucial for teams to triumph in the social media arena. This marks the end of not just this chapter, but also an iterative process that sports franchises must consciously inculcate and adapt as they surge ahead in the digital age.

Chapter 7. Fan Engagement: Transforming Spectators into Brand Advocates

In the realm of sports marketing, mutual engagement between fans and sports teams or athletes has increasingly underpinned successful, dynamic campaigns. Transforming spectators into ardent brand advocates necessitates not just receiving support but also fostering relationships that provide value and generate meaningful interactions, resulting in augmented devotion and emotional investment from fans.

7.1. Engaging Fans: A Strategic Imperative

The advent of social media has reconfigured the traditional spectator-athlete dynamic. Where once fans admired their sporting heroes from a distance, the advent of the digital age has made it possible for them to actively engage with athletes, teams, or brands via various virtual platforms. For sports organizations and persons, this shift is a double-edged sword, presenting both opportunities and challenges. On the one hand, there's now an extensive, more accessible platform for building a community of dedicated fans; on the other, there's a greater expectation for immediate, meaningful interaction between fans and their sports heroes.

The integration of fan engagement strategies into sports marketing campaigns is therefore not an added advantage but a necessity. These strategies can take multiple forms, from personalizing content to optimizing real-time interaction with fans.

7.2. The Power of Personalized Content

In today's digital age, sports marketers have an abundance of data at their disposal. They have the capability to know their fans better than ever before: their demographics, preferences, and online behavior. Personalized content, tailored according to the individual fan's profile, significantly uplifts the fan engagement rate.

Moreover, customized content caters to the emotional connection innate to sports fandom. By delivering personalized messages, sports teams can make fans feel recognized and valued, strengthening their affinity towards the brand. Furthermore, unique customized experiences, such as virtual meet and greets or exclusive behind-the-scenes footage, significantly enhance fans' loyalty.

7.3. Harnessing Real-Time Interaction

Social media platforms allow brands to interact with their fans in real-time, making live sporting events an avenue for engaging interaction. Live tweeting, posting visual content in real-time, and directly responding to fans during games fuels the camaraderie inherent in live sports, converting one-time viewers into committed fans.

Real-time engagement also includes reacting to fan-generated content, such as memes, comments, and other user-generated content. By acknowledging and encouraging fan creativity, sports brands can foster a sense of community and increase brand advocacy among their fans.

7.4. Leveraging Fan Communities and User-Generated Content

The power of fan communities lies in their shared passion for a sporting person or team. Sports marketers can leverage this collective power by creating spaces for these communities to thrive, such as branded Facebook groups or online fan clubs. In these communal platforms, fans create and share content, amplify the brand's voice, influence other potential fans and form an emotional connection with the brand.

User-generated content is a potent tool in a sports marketer's arsenal. Encouraging fans to create and share their content—photos, videos, fan art, or posts—not only casts the brand into wider networks but also makes fans feel like active contributors to the brand's narrative. It creates a sense of shared ownership and affinity that transforms fans into brand advocates.

7.5. Applying Gamification in Fan Engagement

Gamification refers to the incorporation of game elements into non-gaming environments. Sports brands often create virtual fan competitions or offer rewards for fan participation to encourage fan engagement. In addition to enhancing enjoyment, this also instills a sense of achievement among fans, deepening their affinity with the sports brand.

7.6. Building Long-Term Relationship Via Content, Community, and Connectivity

Ultimately, fan engagement involves the strategic combination of personalized content, community construction, real-time interaction, user-generated content, and gamification. These tactics, when executed properly, convert passive spectators into active followers and eventually devoted brand advocates.

Transforming fans into advocates is more than a one-off event; it demands a long-term commitment from sports brands. Through consistent and dynamic interaction, brands can establish meaningful connections with fans beyond the virtual world, building loyalty that endures fluctuating performances and changing trends. After all, in sports more than any other field, it's essential to remember: fans are the lifeblood of the sport and should always be at the heart of any marketing strategy.

Chapter 8. The Digital Playbook: Innovative Techniques in Sports Social Media Marketing

In today's athletic realm, crafting a successful social media marketing approach means moving beyond basic tweets and posts. Like a well-designed game plan, a digital playbook holds the key to unlocking the full potential of social media platforms for sports marketing. Filled with innovative strategies, it is crucial for brand placement, boosting engagement, and creating a meaningful connection with fans. It is in this context that we delve into this topic, exploring the tools, techniques, and tactics that craft successful digital sports marketing campaigns.

8.1. Understanding the Playing Field

The first step in formulating strategy is thorough understanding of the playing field. As with any sport, competitors, infrastructure, and rules vary with each platform. As marketers, we need to be fully versed in the individual strengths and offerings of various platforms such as Facebook, Twitter, Instagram, YouTube, and TikTok, to name a few. The choice of platform can considerably affect the potential visibility, engagement, and effectiveness of a marketing stunt.

Understanding user demographics and behavior on each platform is imperative. Here, data analytic tools play a significant role. By capturing and comprehending user behavioral patterns, we can cater our content and narratives for specific platforms and audiences, thereby increasing the potential for success.

8.2. Content is King

The ethos of 'Content is King' reigns supreme in the digital marketing landscape. For sports, it goes beyond showcasing just the games; it involves bringing the audience closer to the athletes, teams, and the overall excitement on and off the field. The narratives crafted should inspire, engage, and connect with the audience on a personal level.

Fertile grounds for content range from videos of awe-inspiring moments or behind-the-scenes insights, to interviews and Snapchat stories of a day in the life of an athlete, or infographics and statisticians' deep dives on Instagram. The possibilities are boundless, and the right mixture can provide a rich and immersive fan experience, which can lead to increased brand loyalty.

8.3. Leveraging Real-Time Interactions

One of the most powerful features of social media is its capacity for fostering real-time interactions. This can become a sports marketer's secret weapon. Live tweeting matches, hosting Instagram Live sessions with athletes, or real-time snapchats of a game provide fans with an immersive and authentic experience. These moments generate instant buzz, drive engagement, and grow brand affinity.

Interactive content like polls, quizzes, and contests are another great way to boost engagement levels. Not only does this content entertain, but it actively involves the audience, turning them from mere spectators into participants.

8.4. Capitalizing on Key Events

The beautiful yet challenging part of sports is its seasonality, spikes, and ebbs. It is filled with key moments—match days, player transfers, drafts, victories, and even losses. These pivotal events are opportunities to generate content with high emotional resonance impacting the audience's hearts and minds, and subsequently, the brand's bottom line. It demands agility and real-time content creation skills, but the rewards can be worth the effort.

8.5. Harnessing User-Generated Content

Fans are a treasure trove of marketing potential. Their passion, stories, and creativity can be channeled into productive marketing through user-generated content (UGC). Encouraging UGC, like fan-art, reactions, and testimonials, can create a sense of community and foster increased engagement. It also provides a wealth of authentic content, building a strong brand image.

8.6. Optimizing for Virality

In the digital media world, virality can turn a local player into a global phenomenon overnight. Consequently, planning for virality should be a key aspect of any digital sports marketing strategy. It revolves around understanding what grabs audience attention, evokes emotion, and prompts shares. Often, it is an intersection of innovative content, timing, and strategic promotion.

8.7. Being Data-Driven

As much as storytelling is an art, sports marketing is also about being data-driven. In the digital landscape, every interaction creates useful data—likes, comments, shares, views. As marketers, it is crucial to capture, analyze, and gain insights from this data. Tools like Google Analytics and Social Sprout, and metrics like engagement rate, hashtag performance, follower increase, and click-through rates aid in measuring the campaign's effectiveness, ensuring a high return on investment.

As we explore these techniques, it is clear that a digital playbook for social media marketing in sports needs to be dynamic, innovative, and well-planned. It must center on the audience and be driven by engagement, relationships, and data. In a nutshell, it is about playing to the strengths of the digital arena, leveraging its capacity for connection, conversation, and community. It is about losing fear, taking strategic risks, and, more vitally, changing the game of sports marketing.

Chapter 9. The Power of Influencers: Celebrity Endorsements in the Social Age

In the past, celebrity endorsements involved prominent figures within the sports world promoting products through conventional channels, like television, radio, and print advertising. The rise of social media, however, has changed this dynamic, with influencers using their platforms to make real-time, relatable connections with fans. These influencers range from renowned athletes to online personalities who have built their own followings by creating digital content revolving around sports.

9.1. The Age of Social Media Influence

Social media platforms have magnified the power of celebrity endorsements by contextualizing communication within the digital sphere and enabling streamlined promotion and interaction. Consumers look up to athletes and other sports personalities for inspiration and entertainment, which influences their behavior, including purchasing decisions and brand perceptions. Social media provides a platform for direct and personalized communication between influencers and their audiences, making the endorsement more credible and impactful. Real-time updates, comments, shares, and likes have made fans active participants rather than passive audiences, amplifying the scope and reach of these endorsements. Instagram, Twitter, and YouTube, among other platforms, have turned into bustling marketing arenas, each with a distinctive environment and preferences.

9.2. Building Influence Strategies

Crafting an effective influencer marketing strategy involves comprehensive understanding. This includes rich insights about the target audience's demographics, psychographics, and behavioral trends. Factors such as influencer-selection, content, timing, platform, feedback mechanisms, and assessment tools also play a crucial role. It's a delicate balance of enhancing the influencer's authentic voice while efficiently aligning it with the brand's message and ensuring the audience resonates with it.

Influencer collaboration should not appear as a mere business transaction; instead, it should be a mutually beneficial relationship where the influencer is also a stakeholder. The narrative of the brand should be seamlessly integrated into the influencer's personal stories, transforming promotional content into everyday conversations. Fan engagement initiatives presented by influencers can create amazing opportunities for brands, making the audience feel like part of the influencer's journey.

9.3. Best Practices in Influencer Endorsements

Best practices for influencer endorsements in sports marketing hinge on authenticity, alignment, engagement, and adaptation.

Authenticity reigns supreme in this digital era, with consumers prizing genuine interactions with their idols. Influencers, therefore, have a higher impact when they partner with brands they are passionate about.

Alignment is a key factor, with the influencer's persona and values needing to resonate with the brand's image. This harmony not only enhances credibility but also fosters stronger connections between the influencer, brand, and audience.

Engagement is crucial since social media thrives on active interaction. Regular updates and responsiveness can fuel the relationship, while contests, live sessions, and other interactive initiatives keep the audience's interest piqued.

Adaptation, finally, refers to the ability to reinvent and evolve with trends, platform features, and audience interests, ensuring that the endorsement strategies are always fresh and compelling.

9.4. Measure Success: The Role of Analytics

The effectiveness of influencer endorsements can be evaluated via the use of analytics and KPIs that demonstrate performance. Engagement rates, follower growth, conversion rates, and sentiment analysis help brands understand the impact of their collaboration. Industry benchmarks and competitor analysis can also provide valuable insights to tweak and optimize strategies. This continual improvement process sharpens the campaign's effectiveness over time, ensuring success and creating a win-win proposition for the brand and the influencer alike.

9.5. Conclusion: The Way Forward

Social media has revolutionized the power dynamics of sports marketing, with influencers playing a transformative role in the realm of celebrity endorsements. This digital turn empowers sports personalities to expand their influence beyond their professional achievements, turning them into influential figures who shape consumer behavior and trends. The strategic use of influencer endorsements can fuel brand growth. However, achieving this requires an ongoing commitment toward understanding and adapting to the evolving digital landscape while staying focused on authenticity, engagement, alignment, and constant measurement and validation. It's an exciting playing field, filled with opportunities, challenges, and rewards, and it's just getting warmed up.

Chapter 10. Measuring Success: Analytics and KPIs in Sports Social Media Marketing

In this ever-evolving world of social media in sports marketing, there remains one constant necessity: the evaluation of success. As teams, athletes and organizations pour effort and resources into their online branding, it's vitally important to measure the efficacy of these exploits. This chapter deliberates on the potent tools of analytics and key performance indicators (KPIs) in sports social media marketing, underlining their roles in improving marketing strategies and ensuring desired results.

10.1. The Importance of Analytics and KPIs

When navigating the expansive ocean of social media, metrics and KPIs work as a compass, directing brands towards their destined marketing goals. They are pivotal in understanding audience engagement, tracking the progress of campaigns, and making data-driven decisions. These tools essentially guide brands in adjusting their marketing sails to ride on the waves of success.

Analytics provide a detailed look into the demographics of the audience. They reveal who is interacting with the content, what they love about it, and when they are most likely to engage. This knowledge is beneficial in crafting content that resonatively appeals to the target audience.

KPIs, on the other hand, are measurable values that demonstrate how effectively a brand is achieving its key objectives. They play a crucial role in determining the effectiveness of a campaign and indicating areas of improvement.

10.2. Choosing the Right Metrics and KPIs

Determining the correct set of metrics and KPIs is a decisive factor in the triumph of a social media strategy. There are a plethora of potential performance metrics available, each offering different insights. The selection should primarily align with the brand's unique strategic goals.

Some commonly used metrics in sports social media marketing include:

- Follower growth rate: This is an indicator of the brand's expanding influence and can help to understand which content or campaign is attracting new followers.

- Engagement rate: This refers to likes, shares, comments, and other forms of user interaction with the content. It provides an overview of how actively users are engaging.

- Reach and impressions: These metrics account for the number of people who see the content and how many times it shows up on users' screens respectively.

- Referral traffic: Insightful about how much of the website or app traffic is sourced from social media platforms.

In addition to these, brands should identify KPIs relevant to their specific objectives. If the aim is increasing ticket sales, the KPI should perhaps be the 'conversion rate of ticket purchase through social media posts or ads'.

10.3. Analytical Tools for Success

Access to the right tools can simplify the complex task of gathering, analyzing, and interpreting social media metrics. Many platforms, like Twitter Analytics and Facebook Insights, provide built-in functionality for tracking metrics. Services like Google Analytics offer more advanced tools to track social media-driven website traffic.

Comprehensive social listening tools such as Hootsuite, Mention, or Sprout Social deliver wide-ranging insights into brand mentions, sentiment analysis, competitive analysis, and much more.

10.4. Beyond Quantitative Analysis – Qualitative Measures

While the numerical data derived from metrics and KPIs is crucial, it doesn't disclose the complete picture. Qualitative analysis plays an integral role in understanding the fans' emotive connection to the content. It delves into user comments, reviews, and shared reactions to capture underlying sentiments. Emotional analysis enhances the understanding of content perception, thereby informing how to create narratives that emotionally resonate with audiences.

10.5. The Road Forward: Predictive Analysis in Sports Marketing

Looking towards the future, predictive analytics unveils new possibilities. Employing AI and machine learning algorithms, it can discern patterns in past data to forecast future trends. For sports marketing, this could mean predicting fans' response to specific content or anticipating the next big trend in fan engagement.

In conclusion, the combination of analytics and KPIs in sports social media marketing enables brands to stay attuned to their audience, measure their marketing efforts, and continually refine their strategies. By upholding a strong focus on both data-driven and qualitative approaches, they can hit the bullseye in the complex, fast-paced game of social media sports marketing. Through employing predictive analytics, they can even secure a strategic advantage in the competitive field, always staying one move ahead.

Chapter 11. The Playing Field Ahead: Future Trends in Sports Marketing

The latitude of exploration in sports marketing is expanding hastily as we dive deeper into the age of social media. This chapter dissects future trends in the industry, promising a glimpse into tomorrow's landscape, where technology and creative marketing tactics intertwine to redefine the traditional domains of promotion. As communication mediums continue to evolve and consumer behavior transforms drastically, future trends in sports marketing will reflect these changes, delivering a panorama teeming with novelty and dynamism.

11.1. Harnessing the Power of Artificial Intelligence

Artificial Intelligence (AI) will redefine the sports marketing industry. AI-driven technologies, including chatbots, predictive analytics, and personalization algorithms, will streamline audience targeting, content creation and delivery, and customer service. AI chatbots can ensure personalized and consistent fan experiences, answering queries and providing information promptly. Predictive analytics, powered by machine learning models, will make future campaigns far more strategic and targeted. They will leverage historic fan data to predict behaviors and preferences, enabling brands to create custom-tailored content that resonates deeply with their audience.

11.2. Embracing Virtual and Augmented Reality

Virtual Reality (VR) and Augmented Reality (AR) are set to introduce new dimensions to sports marketing. Immersive experiences offered by these technologies will allow fans to experience games as if they were physically present, thus making them feel more connected with their teams. Brands will utilize VR and AR to create interactive advertisements, allowing fans to literally step into their stories. These technologies will blur the boundaries between real and virtual, capturing fans' imaginations and offering them unforgettable experiences.

11.3. The Rise of User-Generated Content

User-generated content (UGC) is gaining importance in the marketing playbook. UGC paves the way for fans to become more actively involved in their favorite sports brands' promotional journeys. By encouraging fans to share their experiences, brands not only foster deeper engagement but also enhance their credibility. Fans trust content created by their peers more than traditional advertising, making UGC a powerful tool for brand promotion and reputation management.

11.4. The Emergence of Micro-Influencers

In the epoch of social media, influencers have branded themselves as effective marketing channels. The future, however, will witness the rise of micro-influencers. While boasting fewer followers than their mainstream counterparts, micro-influencers generate high engagement rates due to their dedicated and intimate fanbases. As trust in traditional advertising dwindles, micro-influencers provide brands with a more authentic and relatable avenue to connect with their target audience.

11.5. Shifting Gears Towards Sustainability

Sustainability will play a pivotal role in future sports marketing strategies. As environmental consciousness gains traction, sports brands will need to demonstrate their commitment to sustainable practices. Green marketing will ascend beyond a buzzword to a required facet of a brand's marketing strategy. Brands endorsing eco-friendly practices, endorsing environment-friendly products, and sponsoring relevant causes will capture hearts and sway public perception in their favor.

11.6. Amplifying Fan Engagement Through Gamification

Gamification is an emerging trend set to drive fan engagement through the roof. The principles of game design will be applied to non-game elements like promotions and campaigns, introducing a fun, competitive element that encourages fan participation. Rewards, badges, leaderboards, and interactive challenges will entice fans to engage actively with brands and share their experiences on social media.

11.7. The Shift to Over-the-Top Streaming Platforms

As the cord-cutting trend accelerates, Over-the-Top (OTT) media services will become an essential platform for sports broadcasting. Brands will shift their focus to these streaming platforms, sponsoring and advertising on them to reach out to the continually growing viewer base. This platform shift will demand a rethinking of content strategy to maximize audience engagement on these platforms.

In conclusion, the future of sports marketing inches towards an innovative and highly engaging landscape marked by rapid technological advancements. The smart adoption and implementation of these trends will be key to staying competitive and driving unprecedented fan engagement. How these trends play out will undeniably pave the way for captivating dialogues and experiences between sports brands, athletes, and their ardent fans.

www.ingramcontent.com/pod-product-compliance
Lightning Source LLC
Chambersburg PA
CBHW062305290526
45794CB00006B/2700